Introduction

Pathways in Prayer is intended to provide a practical manual for individuals and groups. We have hopefully designed the material so that it works well employed within the context of a homegroup or prayer cell. It is equally capable of being used to enrich the personal prayer life of the individual Christian.

Obviously, not every aspect of prayer is covered. However, for those who desire to etablish a regular and effective prayer life this is the manual. Katey and I have discovered the benefits of such a prayer life over the years. Although the pattern of our life has altered at regular intervals, we have successfully maintained our prayer walk by applying the principles laid out in this book. And enjoyed doing so!

Preparation, as ever, is the key to making the most of this material. If it is to be used by a group, each group member should have their own copy and prepare by reading the appropriate section prior to the group meeting. Group leaders should carefully consider how best to generate discussion around the various subjects. Time should also be left for questions.

Being resident in the UK, our illustrations and stories/examples predominantly reflect that background. However, we trust this will not prevent anybody of any nationality from enjoying the contents.

It is our prayer that use of this manual will provoke an outbreak of prayer which, in turn, will be the means of the grace and goodness of God breaking out across the face of the earth.

Mike and Katey Morris

1
The Importance of Prayer

George Müller, a fine Christian who lived between 1805–1898, was renowned for the orphanages he started. He was a man known for the quality of his faith and prayer.

In over sixty years his orphanages cared for almost 10,000 children. Yet no appeal for funds was ever made: each pound received and each staff member recruited was a result of believing prayer. George Müller lived in an attitude of prayer.

His prayers were always answered, though they often required persistence. It is reported that he prayed for a friend's conversion for the whole of his life. However, Müller died knowing that his friend remained outside the Kingdom of God. Yet in the years following Müller's death that friend finally yielded to the Spirit of God and became a Christian.

The story of George Müller illustrates both the power of prayer, that is having a real impact in today's world, as well as the importance of perseverance in prayer: answers are not always immediately forthcoming.

And the essential clue in this story is that prayer can and does work. No matter previous failure, our testimony is that a simple, practical prayer life can be established by everyone. This book is a guide to that end.

Scripture tells us that all manifestations of God are preceded by prayer. The story of Nehemiah rebuilding the walls of Jerusalem is just one example (Nehemiah 1:1 – 2:9). Nehemiah, informed of the situation in Jerusalem, was deeply moved. He wept, mourned, fasted and prayed to God. His prayer involved confession and calling upon God's faithfulness to restore the situation.

In Nehemiah 2:1 we are told the date when he goes before King Artaxerxes. This indicates that from the moment Nehemiah started praying to the time when he had the opportunity of presenting his case to the king, four months had passed. Persevering in prayer is where many of us falter — not so Nehemiah. He went for what he prayed about!

The king, noticing Nehemiah's sadness, asked what troubled him. Because he had been praying, Nehemiah knew exactly what to ask for. With a brief 'arrow prayer' to God (Nehemiah 2:4) he laid out the plan he had carefully crafted in the place of prayer.

The king grants Nehemiah's request. Why? Because prayer has prepared the way. Prayer changes the situation dramatically, and so Nehemiah sets out to fulfil his vision to rebuild Jerusalem's walls. Here is clear evidence of the way in which God acts in response to prayer. *Prayer always precedes the activity of God.*

Sometimes prayer precedes an activity of God which may not be a *direct* answer to those specific prayers — it may be more than we ask or think. In Luke's Gospel chapter nine (verses 28–36), Jesus is praying with Peter, John and James. Suddenly Jesus is transformed and appears with Moses and Elijah. *Once again prayer has preceded the activity of the supernatural in the earth.*

At Pentecost (Acts 2:1–4) we discover that the believers are together in one place, praying constantly (Acts 1:14). As they pray and wait for the promised Holy Spirit, there is a sound like the blowing of a violent wind coming from heaven and they are all filled with the Holy Spirit. *Once again prayer precedes the divine working of God in the earth.*

SEARCH

Look up the following three passages and identify how prayer precedes the activity of God in each situation.

Write down what happens as a result of faithful prayer.

The passages are: Acts 4:23–31, Acts 10:1–48; Acts 12:1–19.

Acts 4:23–31 _____

_____

Acts 10:1–48 _____

_____

Acts 12:1–19 _____

_____

FAITH IS THE KEY

However, our problem is that our personal experience of prayer is generally not the same as the exciting stories we read in Scripture. We have a much poorer prayer experience. Perhaps we have prayed in all sincerity for someone's health to be restored, only to see them deteriorate. Or we have prayed with all the power we can muster for the salvation of a friend, and yet they seem to drift further away from God's Kingdom. Every time we fail to see a prayer answered our confidence is challenged.

Why continue to pray? Often it is because we have been taught that we ought to pray, that it is part of the Christian's duty to pray. However, unless that prayer is made in faith, enjoying a measure of conviction that God can and will intervene, then it is no more than an empty religious duty and as such is worthless. The book of Hebrews tells us that without faith it is impossible to please God (Hebrews 11:6).

The Bible constantly confirms that we worship a God who answers prayer. If prayer involves God's will being done on earth, as it surely must, then we need to pray with the conviction that this will indeed happen.

SEARCH

Take a few minutes to look up the following verses: Mark 11:22–26; Luke 11:9–13; John 14:1–14; John 16:23–24.

Write down your answer to the following question:
What does Jesus promise that God will do in response to our prayers?

_____

_____

_____

Paul summarises this in 2 Corinthians 1:20: "For no matter how many promises God has made, they are 'Yes' in Christ. And so through him the 'Amen' is spoken by us to the glory of God. Now it is God who makes both us and you stand firm in Christ. He anointed us, set his seal of ownership on us, and put his Spirit in our hearts as a deposit, guaranteeing what is to come."

YES AND AMEN

How should we proceed? We have a choice to make — do we want to live biblical or unbiblical lives? What is your answer?

We cannot be those who accept the Bible with our minds and yet in practice fail to realise its promises. To live like that would cause great instability because there would be a credibility gap — and the divided person ultimately becomes unstuck!

Therefore, we must make a choice. If we choose to live content with an experience of unanswered prayer, then we must reduce God's Word to the level of our experience. That means explaining away the power of God so that we can live comfortably with our lack of experience in answers to our prayers. Alternatively, if we can agree that our prayer experience is poverty stricken, we can tell God we want our lives to be brought into line with His eternal Word as revealed in Scripture.

This is what Katey and I decided to do. We made an agreement with God, saying "In spite of the lack of answers to our prayers, we want to put our hands into Your hand, and allow You, Father God, to bring our lives into line with Your Word. We want to become biblical Christians."

Since that time, both Katey and I have prayed for many people and situations. Sometimes we have seen God answer prayers instantly. On other occasions it has taken a period of time before we have seen answers to prayer. In other situations, although we have prayed frequently, we still await the fruit of those prayers.

" . . . to him who is able to do immeasurably more than all we ask or imagine . . . to him be glory in the church and in Christ Jesus . . . !"

Ephesians 3:20, 21

YES, GOD ANSWERS!

In my early years as a Christian I started to pray for my friends, having a keen desire to win them for Jesus. In particular, I was concerned for a couple of friends whom I visited regularly and with whom I developed a great friendship, but I couldn't work out how to explain the Gospel. One evening before visiting these friends, I prayed specifically that they would be converted that night. I set out quite excited, but when I arrived I was disappointed. The room was full of people — how could I have a serious Gospel chat with that group of noisy revellers in the way?

Eventually, by about 11 pm, the last of the folk had drifted off and I was getting ready to leave myself. I was somewhat frustrated with God, myself, my friends — in fact, everything. Then a chance remark about some world event provoked one of my friends to ask a question begging a Christian response. Once given, it unlocked a floodgate of questions about Christianity, all of which, to my surprise, I was not only able to answer to their satisfaction but was also turning up specific Bible verses to support my case!

After a couple of hours, my friends asked to become Christians and I led them in a prayer of commitment. As I cycled home that night, I was gripped with doubts that they had really come to faith, but they remain Christians to this day. God does answer prayer!

FRIENDSHIP WITH GOD

Prayer is not only about getting the will of God done on the face of the earth. It is also about developing an intimate relationship with Him.

In the Old Testament we discover in Daniel someone who concentrates on proving a faithful friend of God. By remaining faithful in prayer Daniel proved God's faithfulness (Daniel 1:8-16; 6:1-24). And God was able to demonstrate His authority and influence to those in high places. Yet it was costly for Daniel, placing him in apparently difficult and dangerous circumstances. Will we prove faithful friends of God?

When Katey and I were told that medically we had a less than one per cent chance of conceiving a child, we were shocked. We prayed, expecting God to heal us. Yet as we prayed and began to listen, we realised that God wasn't interested in talking to us about our childlessness. He began to put His finger on other areas of our lives. Childlessness became the crucible in which our relationship with God began to grow. Prayer was as much about building a relationship with our Creator as it was about getting things done.

Indeed, we now realise that prayer is a relationship, and just as any relationship grows by means of conversation, so our relationship with God grows through prayer.

THINK

What qualities do you look for in a relationship? Discuss with the group, or think through for yourself and make a list.

_____   _____

_____   _____

_____   _____

Then in two or three sentences describe how you develop these qualities in your relationship with God. What qualities are missing in your relationship with God that you would like to develop?

_____

_____

_____

_____

_____

Write a letter to God telling Him how you would like your relationship to develop. Make it a proper letter, writing about yourself, what you appreciate about God, and what kind of friendship you desire. Now read that letter aloud as a prayer to God.

COMMITMENT

Prayer is about seeing the power of God breaking into the realm of our human realities. Prayer is about a growing relationship with God which demands perseverance. We need to be those who agree to allow our lives to be brought into line with God's Word. Pause and agree to do that now.

Pray aloud:

"I want my life to come into line with Your Word. Father, I place my hand into Your hand and ask that You might bring my experience into line with Your Word, so that I might know and see that the promises of God are indeed 'yes' and 'amen' in Christ Jesus."

 *Prayer Action Idea*

Many of us find difficulties with prayer.

Pause for a moment and list the difficulties you have, e.g. wandering thoughts. Alongside those difficulties set down in writing ways in which you could prevent those difficulties from interfering with your prayer time.

DIFFICULTY	SOLUTION
Wandering thoughts	Use these thoughts as additional prayer fuel before going back to things I was praying about

2

The Lord's Prayer

Good news! Every Christian has trouble with prayer. So don't be discouraged. The disciples who lived close to Jesus also struggled with prayer.

Look up Luke 22:39–46. 1. What did Jesus request of the disciples?
2. In what condition did He find them when He returned? Write out your answer.

1 _____

2 _____

The disciples had been with Jesus for three years. They had lived with Him and learned from Him. They had observed His miracles as well as His close relationship with His Father. But in a moment of pressure they were unable to stay awake and pray as requested. How like us! The good news is that this problem can be changed. And that's the challenge of this workbook.

We live in an age of instant gratification. We know what we want and we want it now. That's why there are miraculous instant weight loss programmes available. A friend of ours embarked on one of these, and it was true that he lost weight very swiftly, but he regained it equally quickly. What was required was a change of lifestyle. It would demand discipline, commitment and perseverance. There was no miracle cure.

And so it is with prayer. In Luke 11:1–4 we discover the disciples asking Jesus for the 'how' of prayer. They have observed Jesus talking with His Father and are keen to pray also. Jesus doesn't give a lecture on the theory of prayer but a guide to its practice. Power in prayer always lies in the practice.

Jesus taught them what we call the Lord's Prayer. Look up the Lord's Prayer in Matthew's Gospel (6:9–13). We're going to work through the Lord's Prayer phrase by phrase — it provides a useful model for prayer and gives a framework for our own prayer life.

PRAISE

"Our Father in heaven, hallowed be Your name."

We begin by reflecting on the Fatherhood of God. Many have had bad experiences of being fathered and have no real intimate knowledge of what it is to have a loving, caring father whose interest is for our success and welfare. However, this is the Fatherhood of God. We recognise that our security is in Him and He has our best interests at heart. We need to pray out of a place of rest and of knowledge that "He who is for us is greater than he that is against us!"

We are also invited to recognise that God is holy, worthy of praise and honour. Indeed, Scripture is full of the praises of God's character and rejoicing in the interventions He has made in the lives of people and nations. It is good that we should take time to give thanks to God for who He is and reflect upon His character. As we do so, we find ourselves uplifted in spirit and realising once again how great is our God and that there is no other God except Him.

To summarise: this phrase invites us to praise and that's where we begin our daily journey of prayer.

THANKSGIVING

1 Look up Psalm 103. Read it and pick out three characteristics about God for which you can give thanks.

1. _____

2. _____

3. _____

2 Write a brief sentence describing God as your Father.

_____

3 Write a short prayer of praise to God and read it to the group or during your church meeting.

_____

_____

_____

_____

PURPOSE

"Your kingdom come, your will be done on earth as it is in heaven."

In this section we begin to pray that God's intentions and purposes might be evident on the face of the earth — as opposed to Satan's intentions and purposes. God has strategies and plans for the benefit of mankind. As His children we are invited to pray in these strategies. And yet, as we will see later, our battle is with Satan who is totally opposed to God's success in this world.

Therefore we begin to consider our own situation, the circumstances within our own local community, our nation and our world, and we pray for the will of God to be done here and now. Scripture is clear that the will of God is done in heaven therefore we can pray with great confidence that God's will — as we understand it to be in heaven — might be done on earth now.

Look up Revelation 21:1–4, 21:6–8; John 3:27–36; 4:21–24; 14:9–14; Matthew 28:16–20; Luke 18:1–8; Job 1, 2:1–10, 42.

It is the business of the church to enable the will of God to be done in the streets, the communities, the nations of the world. It is our privilege to identify key areas such as education or deprivation where we might pray very specifically for God's will to be done.

One word summarises this phrase: it is **purpose.**

PROVISION

"Give us today our daily bread."

This phrase invites us to call upon God for our personal daily provision. This is the urgent prayer of God's servant who must be ready to serve wherever God calls. The Bible reveals that God's people have always been dependent upon God's provision to enable them to fulfil the purpose of His Kingdom. Later on in the same chapter Jesus reminds His disciples not to worry about the future.

Memorise Matthew 6:34.

In seeking first the kingdom of God we must look to God for each day's needs. This challenges our western, materialistic mindset, conditioned as it is to income levels and financial security.

I have had the privilege of travelling into a number of countries where Christians suffer for their faith. I call it a privilege because it is remarkable to see both the level of faith they have that God provides, and their great generosity in feeding and caring for visitors. It would appear that during such visits their hospitality is given out of what they don't have rather than the abundance of what they do. This leaves a deep impression.

*One word summarises this phrase. It is **provision**.*

TAKE STOCK

1 Make two lists of the things you have, under two titles, a) essentials, b) non-essentials. Consider how much time is taken up with the non-essential things.

ESSENTIALS	NON-ESSENTIALS
_____	_____
_____	_____
_____	_____
_____	_____
_____	_____

2 Write a prayer requesting God to provide for the real needs you currently have.

_____

_____

3 Identify the needs of your family and friends. Write them down and then pray for them.

FAMILY	FRIENDS
_____	_____
_____	_____
_____	_____
_____	_____

PARDON

"Forgive us our debts, as we also have forgiven our debtors."

Christianity is based upon relationship. From before the creation of the world God the Father, Son and Holy Spirit lived together in harmonious relationship. When Jesus visited the earth as man and God, He made relationship with God available to man once again, through His death on the cross and resurrection. We have the graphic illustration of the curtain in the Temple being ripped in two from the top to the bottom, signifying God's forgiveness available to man.

Jesus' own teaching spoke clearly of the need to forgive. Not just once or twice, Jesus' suggestion was seventy times seven (Matthew 18:22). That's really an infinite amount of forgiveness.

We must forgive one another constantly. There is no room for grudges or bitterness towards someone. In Matthew 5:23–24 Jesus makes it clear that even when we feel that we are right, if we are aware that our brother may have something against us, it is we who should take the initiative. Remember God took the initiative in dealing with the sin problem and restoring our relationship with Himself and we must be a people who initiate forgiveness.

This phrase reminds us that the measure we forgive will be the measure by which we are forgiven. As pardoned sinners we know that Christ has given all for us. Outside of Christ we are nothing. We, therefore, have no ground to stand on in refusing to forgive those who have hurt us. By living in right relationship with God and with one another we create an openness and an honesty through which we can encourage and affirm one another and so bring in the Kingdom of God.

*One word to summarise this phrase is **pardon.***

ACTIVITY

1 List anyone with whom you have broken a relationship. Pray for forgiveness for that broken relationship and for God's blessing on that person. Discuss with the group any difficulties or questions this produces for you.

_____

_____

_____

2 Ask God's forgiveness for ways you have failed to represent Him the best way you can, both privately and publicly.

3 Think of work, social and family life. Write down how you could better represent the Kingdom of God in these environments.

_____

_____

PRESSURE

"And lead us not into temptation, but deliver us from the evil one."

Here we ask God to direct us away from things which cause us to sin and to guard us from traps set by the enemy. In 1 Peter we are reminded that Satan is "like a roaring lion prowling around looking for whom he may devour" (1 Peter 5:8).

A couple of years ago we were on safari and were driven out to a kill. The lions guarded the carcass by day and fed by night. We took great care travelling to the kill because lions are powerful animals and we didn't want to upset them! Similarly, we ask God to protect us from walking into enemy traps aimed at compromising our faith.

When we are under pressure, such as a time of sickness, we pray that God would keep us during the time of pressure. Just as God looked after Shadrach, Meshach and Abednego inside the fiery furnace (Daniel 3:14–28), and He sustained Daniel in the lions' den (Daniel 6:16–23), so our God is committed to strengthening us and protecting us in the middle of pressure.

We should pray to be kept strong in times of pressure that God might be glorified. James in his epistle (1:2–3) reminds us to consider it pure joy when we go through trials because the testing of our faith develops perseverance and perseverance produces maturity which glorifies God.

One word to describe this phrase is ***pressure.***

TAKE STOCK

1 Discuss with two others in the group the pressures you find yourself under.

2 Sort them into the following categories: a) peer-group pressure, e.g. fashion, lifestyle; b) personal achievement pressure, e.g. promotion at work; c) spiritual pressure, e.g. compulsive lying; d) specific pressure, e.g. illness.

3 Each person in the group should pray for someone else and their list of pressures, asking God to help them, protect them, strengthen them and lead them away from sin.

 # *Prayer Action Idea*

Use this page to write out your story. By your story I mean how you found God and the story of your walk with Him.

Once you've written it out, get a highlighter pen and highlight all those things God has done for you for which you want to give thanks. When you have completed your list, take time going through it, actually thanking God for all He has done.

_____

_____

_____

_____

_____

_____

_____

_____

_____

_____

_____

_____

_____

_____

_____

_____

_____

Next, think of your life ahead: list three things you'd like God still to do. These may be with regard to your future work, opportunities within church or character development. Once you've listed them, pray about them. Remember to pray regularly for these things.

1 _____

2 _____

3 _____

Now that you have your testimony written out, why not share it with a friend? Our story of how God met with us and how we met God is one of the most powerful ways of influencing people with the Gospel.

3

Prayer as a Lifestyle

If we are to be practical about prayer, we must integrate it as a daily practice in our lives. This is the hard part because every one of us lives differently. Singles live differently to marrieds who, in turn, live differently to families. Shift workers live differently from those who work from nine to five. Whatever your situation, you will have your own specific lifestyle.

If we are serious about being faithful in prayer, we will find that it is best expressed through our natural, everyday lifestyle.

MAKING A START

Initially, if you are not used to praying regularly on your own, find someone else (same sex) in your church with whom you can pray at least once a week. Don't be over-enthusiastic. Select half an hour at a time of the day which is mutually convenient to you both and come together TO PRAY.

SEARCH

Look up the following verses in Mark's Gospel and discover how Jesus made time for prayer:

Mark 1:12–13; 1:35–37; 2:13; 3:7; 3:13; 6:30–33; 6:45–46; 9:2–10.

First, identify a number of issues to pray about. These could include personal and family concerns, requests for prayer from other church members, and other issues which are important to you.

Before you begin, take time to reflect upon those issues for which you want to give thanks to God. Praising Him enables us to lift our sight to realise afresh who God is and what He has already been doing in our lives.

Having talked through these things, briefly pray through the issues, being sure to conclude at the end of the half hour as you agreed. Alternatively, you may prefer to explain one issue, pray for it, and when you feel you have prayed sufficiently for that concern (after five or six minutes perhaps) then introduce a new area and pray for that. Develop a programme and a process which you feel comfortable with.

If you are praying on your own, adopt a similar pattern. Remember, if you have not been praying regularly then it is ridiculous to assume you will be able to spend an hour in prayer. Start by taking 15 minutes and try to sustain an effective 15 minutes of prayer. *Bad experience leads to bad practice.*

PRAYER AS A LIFESTYLE

For some of us, sitting in our bedrooms or front rooms is not the ideal place to pray. Our minds wander, the chair is so comfortable that we fall asleep, or we are constantly interrupted by people passing through!

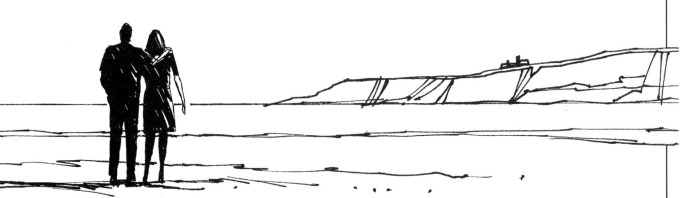

Katey and I like to pray as we walk either by the sea or on the Sussex Downs — a privilege of living on England's south coast! There is nothing unbiblical about this; the important thing is to find the places where prayer works for us. This needs to be incorporated into our lifestyle, and the more this happens the more effective our prayer life will become.

For every one of us each day has different demands. It might be shopping one day, visiting the dentist another. However, there is a pattern for most of us around which we fit such necessities. Overleaf you will find a chart in which you should fill in the regular pattern of your life as best you can.

These patterns are the habits of our lives; when we get up in the morning, when we stop for a cup of tea or coffee, when we lunch, when we take a break, when we walk the dog or stroll to the shops. Prayer needs to be adopted into the regular rhythm of our lives. So when you have filled in the details of your habitual pattern, slot in prayer at convenient times and incorporate it in your weekly rhythm.

Pray while you walk the dog, or clean the house, or collect the children from school; while queuing at the Post Office, or travelling on the bus. Pray everywhere — even if it is only for a couple of minutes. And if you can't think of what to pray, then give thanks to God for who He is.

PRAYER ABOUT YOUR LIFESTYLE

1. Location

Since prayer is part of our lifestyle, we need to introduce God into our decision-making as individuals, as couples, as families. We need to ask God where we should be living.

So often career moves determine our geographical location. But if we are those who are seeking to bring in the Kingdom of God, we must first consider God's agenda for us. We are servants of God and of nobody else.

At times that may mean we need to take costly decisions over location; perhaps remaining where we are, putting first our local church and community commitments rather than following that lucrative career move.

2. Work

When we come to choosing jobs, we need to ask whether it is God's job for us. What are the factors that have convinced us that this is what God has really called us to?

We need to be those who know the calling of God no matter what we do. It has become popular to think that the word 'calling' is only associated with what are termed full-time Christian workers. This is a nonsense. Every single one of us must be called to the work we are doing, and feel comfortable that Jesus is using us in it and that we are serving His interest.

	Monday	Tuesday	Wednesday	Thursday	Friday	Saturday	Sunday
6 – 8							
8 – 9							
9 – 11							
11 – 13							
13 – 14							
14 – 16							
16 – 17							
17 – 18							
18 – 19							
19 – 22							
22 – 24							

3. Love

Have you asked God about your choice of life partner? Many people's usefulness in God is curtailed by a bad choice made in this critical area of relationships.

TAKE STOCK

For those, who are married:

Ask yourself — Am I provoking my partner to follow Jesus?

List three ways in which this is true, and three ways in which you may be a hindrance. Talk it through together as husband and wife and then pray over each issue and recommit your marriage to God's service.

_____

_____

_____

_____

For those who are unmarried:

Ask yourself — What are my aims in God?

List three aims. If you are looking for a marriage partner, list three characteristics of the sort of partner you are looking for. Do your aims in God match the characteristics you have described for your partner?

AIMS

_____

_____

_____

CHARACTERISTICS

_____

_____

_____

Pray, asking God to provide a partner for you, and listen to what He says. Singleness is not God's second best; it may be His will and purpose to enable you to fulfil your aims.

For the separated or divorced:

Ask yourself — Why did the relationship fail?

List three reasons. Do you still have emotional and spiritual hurts as a result of the relationship? Note them down. Ask God for healing and, if appropriate, invite a close friend to pray with you.

_____

_____

_____

_____

_____

_____

I must ensure my partner loves Jesus more than they love me. I want them to provoke me to press harder after Jesus and to ensure that together our effectiveness for the Gospel will be enhanced. It is essential to think about the backdrop of eternity rather than simply of the short-term benefits of having a friend and lover.

4. Finance

In this age of indebtedness we must involve God in our income and expenditure. If we are under severe financial pressures, we should ask ourselves whether this is something we need to endure, or whether it is something of our own making because we have over-stretched ourselves.

Part of our income needs to be released to ensure the continual growth and development of God's interests and purposes. Indeed, all that we have comes from God and will ultimately return to Him. We ought to be wise and effective stewards of those resources that are entrusted to us. Every penny that we have is God's and we must consult God on its best usage.

TAKE STOCK

Ask yourself the following questions about your location, work and finance:

Am I happy where I live?

☐ Yes ☐ No

_____
_____
_____
_____

Am I happy where I work?

☐ Yes ☐ No

_____
_____
_____
_____

Am I happy with my finances?

☐ Yes ☐ No

_____
_____
_____
_____

Whether the answer is yes or no, list three reasons why. If you are uncertain, identify the reasons for those uncertainties.

Where appropriate talk it over with other group members, then list three prayer requests in the light of your answers to the previous questions. Over the next month pray about these matters — and make a note of what God says to you about them; through Scripture, through talking with a friend or your partner, or directly by a dream or vision or thought He drops into your mind.

Prayer request   **What God has said**

1 _____   _____

2 _____   _____

3 _____   _____

 *Prayer Action Idea*

Prayer Triplets

This has proved a most effective model for praying for people to become Christians. However, it can be used in many other ways.

First of all, you need to find two other people with whom to pray on a regular basis. Once you've identified these two other people, get together and decide on a regular time when you will meet. Ideally, you should meet to pray at least once a week.

Having decided when you will meet, you need to decide *where* you will regularly meet. The best place would be somewhere in easy reach of all members of the group and somewhere where you are unlikely to be disturbed by noise or interruptions.

Next, make an agreement that you will *pray* together for a minimum of 20 minutes. It may sound a long time, but between three of you it will really race past.

Once you have decided when, where and for how long, you need to identify *what* you will pray for. This may vary, but a prayer triplet is an ideal model for praying for unbelieving friends and relatives. Each member of the triplet should write down three names of friends or relatives for whose salvation they wish to pray. That means the group will be praying for nine people to become Christians.

At the beginning of the time you may want to give a little bit of background and introduction to the people on your list so that those praying with you on the triplet can pray with a measure of insight and discernment. But remember to spend a full 20 minutes specifically in prayer!

It's also important to remember that this is not a chance to gossip, but a prayer meeting, and the focus and content of your prayers should be kept confidential between the three of you.

Another area you might like to concentrate on is praying for a deepening of the relationship with God in one another's lives. Or you might have an international focus and identify three nations for which you want to pray. Again, each of you needs to do some background research to help the others in the prayer triplet to pray in a more informed manner.

Prayer triplets have proved a decisive model for seeing vast numbers of men and women become Christians all over the world.

4

Fuelling the Engine

Just as an engine requires fuel to keep it turning, so we need information to enable us to pray effectively. An effective and interesting prayer meeting demands reliable information to maintain momentum.

At a prayer meeting in our own home we discovered the importance of up-to-the-minute news to guide our prayers and keep our enthusiasm.

Our church, "Revelation", was concerned for Romania. With the help of Jubilee Campaign we organised two trips to visit Romanian pastor Petru Dugulescu in Timisoara in the late 1980s. We had to pray that these trips would be allowed since Ceausescu's regime, then in power, was totally opposed to Christianity.

When the team from Revelation reached one of the border crossings, they were turned away and their papers stamped as refused entry. But when they went to another border crossing, despite the paperwork, they were allowed into the country. On the team's return, they gave us up-to-the-minute information about the situation in the country, and guided us to pray along the same lines as the church in Romania.

Pointer

Are there things your church is doing which should be prayed about? Is there a missionary whom you support? Why not write regular letters keeping them informed of life at home and asking for current news from their country? Or link up with a believer overseas as a sort of prayer-pal. Find out the benefits of receiving as well as giving prayer.

Find out what the young people need prayer for in schools and pray regularly for the schools in your area. The story is told that a lady in the United States of America prayed regularly for the children in the school near where she lived. Little did she know that in that school was a boy named George Verwer, who responded to God and established one of the most radical and dynamic modern mission movements, Operation Mobilisation. Prayer precedes the activity of God!

Returning to our experiences in praying for Romania, we remember one Friday morning in December 1989 when the troubles were at their height with Ceausescu. We prayed strongly that Ceausescu would fall, and we received a real sense that something was happening in the spiritual realm. You can imagine the excitement of the prayer group when later that same morning news came through that Ceausescu had fled and the People's Revolution had taken one further step forward.

Another area we invested much prayer in was the whole issue of witchcraft and the occult. We received information that major occult activity was to take place on midsummer's evening on the Downs that surround Chichester. In the light of that information, we called upon God to break in and midsummer's night was a total wash-out. The heavens opened and it rained solidly throughout.

Pointer

Are there unhelpful activities in your neighbourhood? Many have effectively prayed for a reduction in the influence of local occult or sex shops. Or again, they have successfully requested their local newsagent to reduce his stock of pornography, supporting that request in prayer. You could write to your local MP, offering the prayer support of your church; ask for particular areas of concern for which they would appreciate prayer.

Without good and reliable sources of information, it is difficult to pray effectively. Today we are surrounded by suitable sources to fuel our prayers. Let us give you a few suggestions.

Information source one:
The newspaper

Newspapers can be an important stimulus to channel our concerns into effective prayers. Whatever your choice of national newspaper, there will always be headlines which demand prayer. Issues touching on world peace, child abuse, violence on the streets, homelessness — the list is endless.

If we take seriously our responsibility to pray, we will want to pray through the issues behind the headlines. In chapter 33 of his prophecy Ezekiel is warned by God of the importance of the role of the watchman in observing the trends in society. These trends affect people. Likewise, we are called to be modern-day watchmen and women, observing what is taking place and bringing these issues to God in prayer.

ACTION

Get hold of a highlighter pen and read through your newspaper, marking *three* key headlines which grab your attention and interest. Find out where the nation or town is for which you are praying. Take a moment to ask God to speak to you about His concerns about the issue. Be quiet for a short period so that He has a chance to guide your praying! Many newspaper stories run over a few days; make it your business to follow that story and pray daily about it.

You may want to make up overhead projector slides on certain issues so that your weekly church prayer meeting enjoys regular news input on national and international issues. TV news is also a useful source of this type of information. Why not video newsclips or special reports and use them as five minute introductions to prayer? And don't ignore your local newspaper for all the information for prayer about the local area.

Information source two:
Christian organisations

There are many organisations producing material on key issues which we can use to guide our prayers.

For example:

ACET (AIDS Care Education and Training) [1] — dealing both in Britain and overseas with the tremendous needs of those suffering from AIDS;

Care Trust [2] — working on the whole issue of the sanctity of life and dealing with the degradation caused by pornography;

The Shaftesbury Society [3] — doing a tremendous work caring for those with various forms of disability and housing problems;

Tear Fund [4] — relief, rehabilitation and development as well as Christian education and evangelism, primarily in the developing nations;

The Children's Society [5] — working with children, young people and families under pressure.

Why not identify a particular area where you have a personal interest and then contact the relevant society? Details of such societies can be found through the Evangelical Alliance, [6] or for information on evangelism worldwide contact the Evangelical Missionary Alliance [7] (or find similar information through articles and adverts in the Christian press).

In this way you can take an issue in which you have a personal interest, and it can become a source of major personal prayer. Thus, our own ability to serve such an area is increased. Many who began praying like this have found God involving them more and more deeply in personal service in such areas.

Information source three:
Leisure reading and television

Many of us regularly read during our leisure time, and ladies' magazines and special interest journals can provide further pointers to what is happening in our society. This is also true of the programmes on our televisions.

In particular, you can identify trends amongst young people, in areas of business and industry and the like. If we believe that God wants to influence every area and sector of life, we should use this information as essential prayer fuel.

For example, what are new mothers being encouraged to do with baby? What are teenage children reading, and what ideas are being sown into their understanding? What are the latest high-tech developments in the computer world?

We can turn our leisure reading into strategic prayer fuel and pray God's heart and mind into the circumstances. One immediate way of working this out is to pause as you read certain articles and send up a few arrow prayers to God before continuing to read.

Information source four:
The rest of the world

It is very easy whilst living in a relatively affluent society to forget we are part of a very large world in which many people do not enjoy the benefits that we do. For example:

- More than 40,000 youngsters under the age of five die in the world every day from preventable diseases.
- Every day 150 million under five's suffer from malnutrition, 23 million from severe malnutrition.
- Every day more than 100 million children of school age never step inside a classroom — 60% of them girls.
- Every day more than 30 million children live on the streets.
- Every day about seven million people are refugees from war or famine.
- By the year 2000 in central and east Africa 10 million children will have lost at least one parent to AIDS.

That's six days prayer fuel alone in these statements!

We cannot forget that God is concerned for the whole world, and that every human is created in His image. And although we may not find ourselves on jumbo jets flying to distant shores, we can still get involved by prayer and affect the conditions in which people live around our world.

— Sign up with an international Christian agency to get prayer information. Most daily newspapers also have international sections. These provide good background prayer information.

— Get hold of a world map and discover where countries are.

— The book *Operation World* by Patrick Johnstone (STL/WEC) provides a marvellous country by country analysis for prayer and information. Get hold of a copy and begin to learn about the world in which we live.

Use such sources of information to enlarge the vision of your local church. Adopt a country, write to its embassy requesting general information. Find out more about it from an agency like Tear Fund. Pray for its government and its people. Develop an informed prayer group in your church for that nation.

Information source five:

Why not consider becoming a personal member of the Evangelical Alliance [6] or the evangelical fellowship in your nation? In Britain the EA — which is happy to service overseas members — produces a member's magazine, containing stories and information about what God is doing across Britain and overseas, and how we can pray for those particular items. There is also a prayer line for current information. And through the EA's Prayer Secretary you could be put in touch with a network of existing prayer groups that exist in the UK, or get information about international prayer networks.

CWR's *Revival* [8] magazine is another regular source for informed praying on important national and international issues. As well as articles, it contains *Prayer Focus*, a digest of current issues and initiatives, to pray through day by day.

FILLING UP WITH FUEL

Work through this checklist and write in the sources of information to which you will now turn to gather sufficient prayer fuel.

1 Which national or local newspaper do I read?

_____

2 What issues am I particularly interested in?

_____

3 What Christian societies represent those interests?

_____

4 What magazines or journals do I read and what is their major focus of interest?

_____

5 What other countries am I particularly interested in or would I like to discover more about?

_____

You might also like to organise a prayer questionnaire for your local church. As well as praying around the world, there are many prayer needs in our local churches. Photocopy the questionnaire overleaf and gather prayer fuel. You could do it over coffee at the end of a Sunday service, or as people leave to go home, or make it a focus for prayer in the middle of a meeting.

Make sure you pray personally and as a church for these items over a month and then repeat the exercise. Hopefully, you will receive testimony of answered prayer *en route*. This is a great means of stimulating prayer interest in your local church.

FOOTNOTES

1. **ACET**, PO Box 1323, London W5 5TF.
2. **Care Trust**, 53 Romney Street, London SW1P 3RF
3. **The Shaftesbury Society**, 18-20 Kingsdon Road, South Wimbledon, London SW19 1JZ.
4. **Tear Fund**, 100 Church Road, Teddington, Middlesex TW11 8QE. **Tear Australia**, PO Box 289, Hawthorn, Victoria 3122.
5. **The Children's Society**, Edward Rudolf House, 69-85 Margery Street, London WC1X OJL.
6. **Evangelical Alliance**, Whitefield House, 186 Kennington Park Road, London SE11 4BT. *Australia:* **The Evangelical Alliance**, PO Box 289, Hawthorn, Victoria 3122.
7. **Evangelical Missionary Alliance**, Whitefield House, 186 Kennington Park Road, London SE11 4BT.
8. **Revival**, CWR, Waverley Abbey House, Waverley Lane, Farnham, Surrey, GU9 8EP.

Questionnaire

Name: _____

Personal items you would like prayer for?

_____

_____

_____

_____

Any family members, neighbours and friends who need prayer?

_____

_____

_____

_____

Any special concerns in your street?

_____

_____

_____

_____

What would you most like God to do?

_____

_____

_____

_____

 *Prayer Action Idea*

Prayer scatter-board

Many people have a cork or hesian-backed notice board in their kitchen or entrance hall. Odd bits of paper, phone numbers you wish to remember and other such information collects, often to a great-depth, on such notice boards!

We have found it useful as a prayer reminder board. We pin up pictures of people we wish to remember to pray for, or campaigning leaflets concerning someone who is in prison for whose release we are praying.

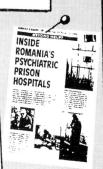

INSIDE ROMANIA'S PSYCHIATRIC PRISON HOSPITALS

We have found the prayer scatter-board a very useful way of reminding ourselves to issue the occasional arrow prayer for a particular person, situation or campaign. Make sure the scatter-board is in an area of the house you pass regularly. The kitchen is ideal; whenever you are making a drink or sitting down for a quick bite something on the scatter-board will catch your attention and you can pray for that situation. Alternatively, the entrance hall is a good place; whenever you leave the house you can look at an issue and pray for it as you leave the house and make your way to the next destination.

Whenever Mike travels overseas for his work with the Evangelical Alliance, he brings back a bank note from the country he has visited and pins it up as a reminder to pray for that nation and for the people that he has met there. You might like to cut out headlines, or maps and photos from the newspapers and pin them up to remind you to pray for a particular country or particular issue over a period of time.

Set up a prayer scatter-board in your home.

5

The Difficulties with Unanswered Prayer

At the time of writing we have been married for nearly 13 years. Although we would love to have a family of our own we remain childless, and the medical judgement is that we have less than a one per cent chance of conceiving a baby. We have prayed continually over that period that God would grant us children.

We believe that God intends human kind to be fruitful and to produce children. We continue to put our faith in God's Word. We continue to pray and yet we have no evidence that God has heard our prayers.

We have cried out to God in anger and grief, yet we must remember that we are instructed to pray constantly and to give thanks in all circumstances (1 Thessalonians 5:16-18).

TAKE STOCK

Make a list of current difficult circumstances in your life.

_____

_____

_____

_____

_____

_____

Are you praying about these things:

     A regularly? ☐

          B irregularly? ☐

               C not at all? ☐

Are you giving thanks:

     A regularly? ☐

          B irregularly? ☐

               C not at all? ☐

Work through the difficult circumstances you have listed and identify how often you are going to pray and give thanks to God over these individual circumstances.

The freedom God allows us enables each one of us to make choices in times of difficulty. It is easy for bitterness or anger to creep in and rob us of our love for God, or our love for ourselves and, hence, our love for others. Indeed, our choices will seriously affect our relationships, enhancing or destroying the quality of our discipleship.

In all circumstances we must take our stand on what we know about God. This is evident through His Word. We need to listen for God's voice to address specific situations and then pray in line with what God says. Often this is the real arena for spiritual warfare.

Whilst many of us accept in principle the truths about spiritual warfare, we still feel as though the carpet has been pulled out from under our feet when things cause us disappointment. We discover that we are not living out of the spiritual resources we have invested in over the years. We go to pieces and behave as though we are not friends of God at all.

VISION

Look up Ephesians 2:4–7.

1. Write out these verses in your own words and then pray your way through them.
2. How should we see the circumstances of our lives?

1 _____

_____

_____

_____

_____

2 _____

Our prayer is really about maintaining a relationship with God; a relationship which enjoys all the benefits for which Christ paid on the cross. No matter what we face or are called upon to endure, we are to continue to build the relationship throughout.

Petru
Dugulescu

Petru Dugulescu — the Romanian pastor mentioned in chapter 4 — was involved in a serious accident when he drove his vehicle across a road junction and it was crashed into by a single-decker bus. Petru, with his arm broken and suffering from shock, immediately gave thanks to God that he was alive, and then turned back to Him to ask, "Why me?"

God instantly reminded him of a recent sermon on the need to continue faithful in spite of our circumstances. He recalled his encouragement to the congregation to recognise their wealth in owning two homes: one in Romania and one in the Spirit. Petru had literally to practise what he had preached; how sometimes we need to turn our gaze away from our earthly habitation and recognise our true position and security in Christ.

It isn't only in Romania that Christians may have to face difficulties. A friend of ours was involved in a car crash which left her in a wheelchair at the age of 18. Having just become a Christian, she talked her situation over with God as she lay in a hospital bed for several weeks. She came to accept her new physical situation while at the same time committing herself to pray for complete healing.

God hadn't said that he would not heal her, and today she continues that prayer from her wheelchair. She is now married to the guy who was with her in that crash, and together they exercise a powerful witness to the grace of God, holding that in tension with an — as yet — unanswered prayer.

Our minds, bodies and emotions can be occupied 24 hours a day with the basic requirements of living, yet we must recognise that we have a home with Christ. There is a place where we can go and walk and talk and refresh our relationship with Him.

THINK

Look up **Hebrews 10:32–39.**

Do you have any complaints to place before God? Perhaps some prayers which remain unanswered, for example? Bring them to God, and tell Him honestly how you feel. Anger is no problem to God. But work it through until you can give thanks even though it hurts. Get to the place where you discover that God loves you and is in charge of your situation.

SEARCH

Read **Hebrews 11**

List the names mentioned in the chapter, and alongside describe the aspects of their lives for which they are commended.

Names: **Commended:**

In your own words, describe the consequences for those who commit their lives totally to following in the footsteps of Jesus.

In times of pressure or difficulty we need to call upon the practical and prayerful support of others in the church. We need to be open, honest and real; truthful about disappointments, fears and anxieties. We must allow the church the privilege of providing the support that is so vital to us at these times. This is the life of the body which Christ entrusted to us by His Holy Spirit.

We should also recall that there is no situation in which Christ will place us which is beyond our ability to endure (1 Cor. 10:13). We need to reflect upon the purpose of pressure in our lives.

Look up Romans 5:1-5:

> *"Therefore, since we have been justified through faith, we have peace with God through our Lord Jesus Christ, through whom we have gained access by faith into this grace in which we now stand. And we rejoice in the hope of the glory of God. Not only so, but we also rejoice in our sufferings, because we know that suffering produces perseverance; perseverance, character; and character, hope. And hope does not disappoint us, because God has poured out his love into our hearts by the Holy Spirit, whom he has given us."*

VISION

List the different characteristics that develop as a result of pressure and suffering. Fill in the blanks:

Suffering produces _____

Perseverance produces _____

Character produces _____

Hope does not disappoint because _____

_____

Can you identify where you are on the list as the result of pressure you have experienced? How does this help you to cope with the tension of unanswered prayer?

_____

_____

Finally, we can recall that Jesus also had to endure difficult circumstances, so when we find ourselves under pressure we are following in His footsteps. And that is an answer to a prayer which many of us have prayed at moments of challenge and commitment.

Write down those prayers which you have prayed which remain unanswered. Next to them identify how often you pray for these things. Be honest: the only person you are trying to fool is yourself if you are not honest in this!

PRAYER   **HOW OFTEN**

_____   _____

_____   _____

_____   _____

_____   _____

_____   _____

_____   _____

_____   _____

Ask yourself whether God has given any indication — through Scripture, or a friend or direct to you — that He will not answer that prayer as you desire? If He has, then write down how and when, then close the door on that request.

But if you haven't had any such indication, then record how you are going to handle the tension between the prayer you have prayed and the fact that to date it remains unanswered. Turn this into a prayer to God.

Look up Philippians 2:1–11, and meditate upon the character of Christ.

 *Prayer Action Idea*

FASTING

Look up **Matthew 4:1–2; 6:16–18; 9:15; Acts 13:2**

In all the above passages you will have found a reference to fasting. What is fasting? Quite simply, it is voluntarily going without food. It is a part of the practice of followers of God throughout history. It is a practice which Jesus Himself followed whilst in the wilderness.

(**Note:** it is going without *food*, not liquid.)

Fasting is a means of setting time aside to make a special appeal to God. It is not intended that you advertise what you are doing (Matthew 6:16-18) but rather you devote yourself to prayer and Bible meditation. The purpose of such a fast can be for greater personal integrity and holiness, for specific issues in our personal lives, the life of our church or the life of the nation, or for the triumph of justice over injustice (read Isaiah 58).

There is no virtue merely in the act of going without food. Rather, it is an agreement with God to see His purposes fulfilled in a given area. It is a personal demonstration of commitment to our verbal prayer, and an act of personal sacrifice.

The early church involved themselves in fasting and it is to be commended as a valid expression of prayer in the church today. However, going without food can be difficult, and certainly if one is aware of a medical condition, one's doctor's advice should first be sought.

As a start, why not identify something you want to commit yourself to pray for as a group or prayer triplet? Agree together to fast for a day, i.e. miss breakfast, lunch and tea. Instead of eating, use that time to pray. It is often fun to break the fast together with a light meal.

6

Spiritual Warfare

Look up Exodus 17:8–13. What were Moses, Aaron and Hur doing as they overlooked the battle?

_____

How and why did Joshua overcome the Amalekites?

_____

How are we to overcome that which opposes God in today's world?

_____

Until we become Christians most of us are unaware of life's spiritual dimension. Some discover it through involvement in the occult or new age. Many others regard talk of occult and spirits as being irrelevant in a sophisticated twentieth-century society.

Yet the Bible is clear: there is a powerful spiritual world in operation, unseen by the human eye. It asserts its influence in the lives of men and women, on peoples and nations.

Search

1 *Look up Ephesians 6:10–18,* and answer the following question:

How does Paul describe the forces that are opposed to those who serve Christ Jesus?

_____

2 *Look up 2 Corinthians 10:3–5.* Against who does Paul say that Christians wage war?

_____

3 *Look up Colossians 2:13–15.* What does Paul say Jesus did after He had died on the cross and risen from the dead?

_____

As Christians we are involved in a real war, facing a real enemy. Yet through Jesus Christ we enjoy a real victory. Satan wants to prevent men and women from discovering the truth about Jesus. He wants to neutralise the effectiveness of the Church. He wants to interfere and do damage in the life of every disciple of Jesus. In a variety of ways he will seek to bring adversity into our lives in an attempt to persuade Christians to lose our affection for Jesus, lose our effectiveness or simply give up.

Search

4 *Look up 2 Timothy 2:3–4.* Paul reminds us that we are called to conflict! It is a part of the commission of every soldier of Jesus.

Let's take a look at this enemy of ours. Called "Satan" in the Scriptures, the word "Satan" means "Accuser". Names were very important in Hebrew, because they described the personality that carried that name. Hence, we know that accusation will constantly come from the lips of Satan. We are to be aware of the difference between conviction of sin which comes from the Holy Spirit and the accusations which come from the lies of Satan.

Conviction will always be very specific. The Holy Spirit always indicates the precise issue with which God wants to deal and we are free to choose whether or not to yield to the prompting of the Spirit.

Accusation, however, is non-specific, leaving the believer feeling out of fellowship with God. Satan constantly tries to bring us down by suggesting that Christianity is a series of laws which we are failing to keep. Hence, we feel bad. Or he constantly reminds us of issues for which we've already repented.

FACE THE FACTS

Fact one:

Satan, also known as Lucifer and Beelzebub, is an angel created by God. He is therefore *not* equal to God. Isaiah 45:5 tells us that no-one is greater than God. There is no God other than the God of Israel, who broke into human life in the person of His Son Jesus who is both human and divine.

Satan is merely an angel who rebelled against God, was defeated and fell from his position in heaven and his role as a servant of God. Since that time he has been the enemy of God and of God's greatest creation, mankind. He tries to prevent man from discovering peace with God.

Look up Luke 10:18; Revelation 12:7–9; Isaiah 14:12.

Write down a list of Satan's characteristics and the details of his rebellion.

_____

_____

_____

_____

Fact two:

Satan is ultimately subject to God's authority. All created beings owe their existence to God. Scripture says that at the end of time Satan will be bound and cast into the Lake of Fire.

In the story of Job Satan only had as much authority as God chose to allow him. Although Job suffered such terrible calamity and personal distress, ultimately he was able to prove the faithfulness and glory of God in the face of Satan's assault. **Read** Job 1, 2 & 42.

Fact three:

Satan was defeated by Christ at Calvary. When he died on the cross and rose from the dead Christ demonstrated His victory.

From this point onwards Satan's power was broken. All the skirmishes which take place from then until Christ's glorious return are merely Satan's attempts to create as much havoc as possible, and to prevent men and women from discovering their true identity and destiny in Christ.

Look up Ephesians 4:8; Colossians 2:13–15; Hebrews 2:14.

Write out the evidence for Christ's victory over Satan.

_____

_____

Fact four:

Satan's tactic is to use reason and logic to convince men and women that he is right and Christ is wrong. He seeks to exploit our emotional weaknesses to turn us against God and to do those things which upset God.

He used reason and logic when he convinced Adam and Eve to sin and break their relationship with God in the Garden of Eden. We also see him using reason and logic when he tries to tempt Jesus in the wilderness.

Look up Matthew 4:1–11, the story of the temptation of Jesus in the wilderness. List the ways Satan tries to cause Jesus to follow him rather than remain faithful to his Father in heaven.

_____

_____

UNDER ATTACK

We have to recognise that Satan is active in attacking individual Christians and the work of Christ on earth. As Christians who are co-operating with God, we will face the principalities and powers, authorities and dominions mentioned by Paul in Ephesians 6:12. In response we must communicate a world view that is based upon God's revelation to us.

Instead of following after the ideas of the world, we are called to change our minds (repent) and begin to think as God thinks. Then we start to see ourselves as God sees us, and commit our allegiance to Him.

Look up Romans 12:1–2.

Here Paul warns the church not to be squeezed into the mould of the world around, but rather to have their minds transformed and to live for Christ.

We need to recognise the corrupting powers that are at work within our society and pray against them, and to pray for those people who are influenced by such powers.

We also need to live godly lives that demonstrate what it is to be a Christian. We need Christians at every level of society. There must be Christian witness, thought and action influencing all society's institutions, from government through industry to local community activities.

THINK

Look up Matthew 5:13–16.

1. What are the properties of salt and light to which Jesus is alluding?

2. How, practically, can we be salt and light at home? at work? at church? with our neighbours?

DOING BATTLE

Principalities and powers are also supernatural forces ranged directly against the Church and individual Christians. In Matthew 17:14–19, as He returns from the Mount of Transfiguration, Jesus is confronted by a boy suffering from epilepsy. Jesus addresses a demon in the boy and commands it to leave him. The boy is healed.

Here Jesus confronts a supernatural spirit which was operating within the boy, apparently causing the boy to suffer from epilepsy. No matter what healing might have been applied by doctors with the cures they had then or indeed today, such medical attention would not have produced the healing necessary, for the boy was actually afflicted by a demonic power.

Such demonic powers have personalities and are personal entities.

Look up Daniel 10:12–14; here Gabriel informs Daniel that God had heard his prayer from the moment it was uttered. However, the answer had been resisted by the spirit of the prince of Persia. Battle had to be done against this power that was resisting a response to Daniel's prayer of faith.

We must recognise that at times there are powers and principalities resisting our prayers, resisting the will of God being done on the earth. This demands persistent and aggressive prayer. Just as Jesus addressed the demonic spirit in the epileptic boy, so we must address the spiritual forces once we have identified who they are.

EQUIPPED TO FIGHT

Finally, God has made provision for us in this realm of warfare. Ephesians 6:10–18 outlines the armour of God. Read those verses and list the various pieces of armour named. Write down alongside each piece of equipment what you think they equate to in the Christian's life as he or she resists the enemy.

Armour

_____   _____

_____   _____

_____   _____

_____   _____

_____   _____

You will note that all the armour God supplies protects the front! God's people are expected to carry the fight to the enemy. If you turn and flee, your back is exposed. Paul reminds his readers that the fight to which we are called is a supernatural one. Without God's provision we should lose. Yet in the spiritual armour outlined (based upon the equipment worn by a Roman soldier), God has supplied us with all we need. It is essential to recognise that there are two words linked with the armour: prayer and requests (Ephesians 6:18). To engage in warfare without effective prayer is to court disaster.

Ask yourself where you feel that the enemy is most successful in defeating you in these areas.

Ask God to fully enable you to withstand the assault of Satan.

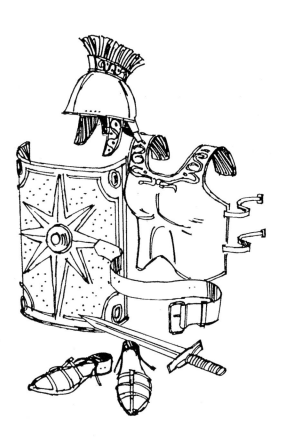

CONCLUSION

So Satan is real. And he wants to do us harm. However, God has already defeated him on the cross and demonstrated His victory through the resurrection. We must adopt a position which makes us aware of Satan's strategies. Before we embark on any activity which promotes God's interests, it is essential that we engage in prayer.

For example, before an evangelistic meeting we must pray for the people participating, for the organisation of the evening and for the salvation of those attending. It is all too easy to arrange a very smooth-running and professional event, but ultimately fail to secure success because of lack of prayer.

One church we knew were planning a major open-air campaign. To run this effectively they set out to hire the local green from the local authority. However, the local authority refused them permission. How many of us would have given up at the first refusal? However, through active spiritual warfare we can overcome Satan's attempts to hinder God's work.

Look up Romans 12:3–5. Satan's greatest strategy is the use of temptation to undermine us. Paul reminds us in this passage not to become big headed. Know your weaknesses. And then avoid them. Joseph fled from Potiphar's wife rather than risk compromise. So we should learn to avoid areas where we know we are weak. As we press on with God, our weaknesses are increasingly addressed and we become stronger in faith and discipleship.

Paul also reminds us that we are not on our own but we belong to the Church. We need each other in defeating Satan. Christianity is not a solo religion. When Jesus went to be with His Father He gave us His Word, His Spirit, and *each other*. The Christian is born for relationships. These relationships provide a secure place in which I can share my weaknesses, receive prayerful and practical support and join with others in the business of spiritual warfare.

Prayer Action Idea

Go on a prayer walk!

Identify the geographical area for which your church has an evangelistic concern. Take a part of that area; the part where you and your family live. On a local map identify a circular walk along the residential areas which will take about 30 minutes to complete.

Decide to walk either with two or three friends or together as a family and set a time when you are going to walk around the circuit praying for your local community. On the day you choose, arrange to meet in your house for 10 minutes of prayer before going out. Having prayed, move out and walk around the streets praying for the goodness and blessing of God on the people whose houses you pass. Don't look suspicious — try not to loiter outside any house, even if you are praying for the people inside!

When you've completed your prayer walk (and it is quite acceptable to pray out loud as you walk along), feedback over a cup of tea any impressions you have that may be helpful for further prayer or which could help those planning evangelistic strategy in your church to understand the community more completely.

Over the last few years *March For Jesus* has developed as a praise march of proclamation and active spiritual warfare. It concentrates on praying for God's will to be done in our towns and cities around Britain.

Why not write off to March For Jesus, (PO Box 39, Sunbury-on-Thames, Middlesex TW16 6PP) and ask for details of a march taking place in your area.

Sometimes these marches have been preceded by prayer walks the length of the country. Get hold of *Prayerwalking,* a book by Graham Kendrick and John Houghton (Kingsway Publishing), which gives details on how to organise a prayer walk within your area.

FURTHER READING

Mike & Katey Morris, *Praying Together*, Kingsway, 1987

John Earwicker, *Prayer Pacesetting*, Scripture Union, 1987

Graham Kendrick & John Houghton, *Prayerwalking*, Kingsway, 1990

Arthur Wallis, *God's Chosen Fast*, Kingsway, 1969